THE LIFE AND T... of GUMMY BEARS

THE LIFE AND TIMES OF GUMMY BEARS

Hans Traxler

HarperPerennial
A Division of HarperCollinsPublishers

FIRST EDITION

LIBRARY OF CONGRESS CATALOG CARD NUMBER 92-56251

ISBN 0-06-095004-8

93 94 95 96 97 **RRD** 10 9 8 7 6 5 4 3 2 1

For Claudia and Iphi,
the natural enemies of Gummy Bears,
who would never have survived
many a trying time without them.

THE LIFE AND TIMES OF GUMMY BEARS

Science has generally come to accept
the "Big Bang" theory of
Gummy Bear creation.

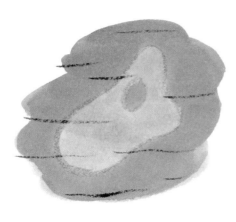

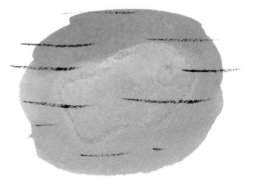

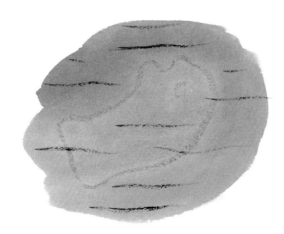

Scientists also agree that it took
3 to 4 million years for microscopic
gumdrops to evolve into fully formed,
air-breathing Gummy Bears.

However, there is still some debate over
whether man descended from the ape
or the Gummy Bear.

The fossil record tells us that there were once many
exotic species of Gummy Bear. Some were 100 feet
long and weighed 50 tons. Others could fly, but
not land. None of these survive.

The Bible tells us that Gummy Bears
faced extinction when Noah couldn't find them
anywhere on his passenger list.

In the Colosseum of ancient Rome,
the cruel Emperor Nero
threw Gummy Bears to the cats.

As Imperial Rome declined, hordes
of Gummy Barbarians overran Europe.

When they first sighted Columbus in 1492,
little did Native American Gummy Bears
realize how much their world
was about to change.

In 1500, Raphael employed two
Gummy Bears as models until their
ridiculously cute expressions
drove him to fire them.

Ivan the Terrible found
Gummy Bears annoyingly hard
to torture.

Although the invention of the
printing press was a boon to humankind,
it could be quite harmful to hapless
Gummy Bears.

Henry VIII was not amused
by his Gummy Jester,
and it lost its head.

Few Americans are aware of the
part Gummy Bears played in the struggle
for independence.

After a mutiny on the high seas, one Gummy Bear
was marooned on a desert island.
It waited patiently for rescue, which came,
quite promptly, 27 years later.

For years, Walt Whitman lived
with a red Gummy Bear who found certain
passages from *Leaves of Grass*
deeply moving.

20

In the Old West, Gummy Bear ambushes
were the scourge of careless cowpokes.

Because of their discretion, Gummy Bears
were much in demand as guards
for the harems of the Ottoman Empire.

In 1880, an intrepid Gummy Bear fell
into the clutches of a savage band
of licorice whips on the Congo.

As Robert Peary neared the North Pole
in 1909, a blizzard raged,
the temperature dropped to −50°,
and all the sled dogs had been eaten....

Fortunately, he had had the
foresight to pack Gummy Bears,
and they saved his life by
sacrificing theirs.

Long before the Wright Brothers took flight,
a Gummy Bear made the first glider
out of a pair of bat wings.
Sadly, it got stuck on landing and gave up.

Of all the Gummy Bears aboard the
Titanic, only two survived.

In the early years of this century,
the depraved Soho Strangler terrorized
London's Gummy Bear population.

Gummy Bears were a major force
in the Chicago gang wars of the 1920s.

In pre-revolutionary Russia, Gummy Bears
were very powerful. A huge store
in Moscow's Red Square catered especially
to their needs. That store still stands.

The invention of talkies forced
Gummy Bears, with their high, squeaky
voices, out of Hollywood.

Because radar could not detect them,
Gummy Bears were used as spies by both
sides during World War II.

All of Europe struggled to recover after
World War II, but Gummy Bears were
particularly hard hit.

But the postwar economy eventually boomed and, like everyone else, Gummy Bears married and started families in record numbers. Unlike everyone else, though, Gummy Bears couldn't start their families until they figured out how to get down off their wedding cakes.

In the 1960s, many Gummy Bears
tried to find themselves through Eastern
mysticism. Gurus like the
Baba Goose Lamp were all the rage.

Obesity

Fear of Flying

Tennis Elbow

Existential Dread

Living so close to humans,
Gummy Bears share many
of our modern woes.

Gummy Bears Now

Today, Gummy Bears are well-respected members of society. Still, they present us with numerous problems and puzzles, such as the Great Gummy Bear Migration.

When harvest time is over,
Gummy Bears gather for their
long flight south.

Getting over the Rocky Mountains can be
too much for even the hardiest Gummy Bears.
Some prefer to just hitch a ride.

Despite the protests of Gummy-rights
activists, several thousand migrating Bears
get caught in nets strung up by
bird catchers in Tuscany.

Every year, untold numbers of
Gummy Bears end up as pizza topping.

Experienced Gummy Bears prefer to winter
in Provence, where they nest in
the walls of old houses, and charm
the local girls with their chirping.

Increasingly, Gummy Bears are choosing not to migrate
at all. As the first snow falls, they seek a cozy nook where
they can remain forgotten until the spring, when
they—and their new cubs—will emerge.

If living in too confined a space,
Gummy Bears become aggressive and lose
all interest in sex.

On the other hand, when left alone for
too long, Gummy Bears become despondent,
biting their fingernails and refusing
to speak.

The patience and discretion
of Gummy Bears make them excellent
house detectives.

Despite their gooey consistency, Gummy Bears
are extremely trustworthy. The only thing you
have to worry about when buying a used car
from one of them is the sticky seats.

Most Gummy Bears prefer
records to CDs.

The Gummy Quintet has been hailed by
critics for its sweet melodies
and bouncy rhythms.

A Gummy Bear will dissolve in
warm salt water, but that doesn't seem
to stop hordes of them from
heading to the beach every summer.

With proper care, Gummy Bears can live to
a ripe old age. Their advice:
"No alcohol, no smoking, and, above all,
avoid children's birthday parties."

The Afterlife and Times
of Gummy Bears

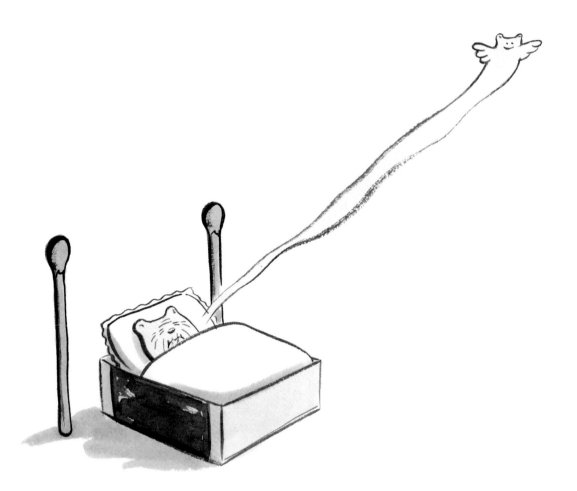

When Gummy Bears know the end is near,
they pack their bags and withdraw
from society. For years,
nobody knew where they went....

Then, in 1935, the explorer B. Nash
found the first of the fabled Gummy Bear
Graveyards while exploring in his greenhouse.

Do Gummy Bears go to Heaven?
To anyone who has gazed at the sky
on a clear night, the answer is obvious.